THE WHEEL OF FORTUNE

THE WHEEL OF FORTUNE

which never fails to answer your Questions

JO SHERIDAN

Designed by ALFRED DOUGLAS

HODDER PAPERBACKS

Copyright © 1970 by Jo Sheridan

Original publication in Great Britain by Hodder Paperbacks 1970

Printed and bound for Hodder Paperbacks Ltd. by
Hazell Watson & Viney Ltd., Aylesbury, Bucks

ISBN 0 340 12522 5

The Oracle of the Wheel has many names. To the Greeks he was Hermes Trismegistus, to the Romans Mercury, while to the ancient Egyptians he was known as Thoth.

Whatever name he travels under, he is one and the same being, the Lord of Luck and Magic, the link between mankind and the gods, the Walker on the Winds.

INSTRUCTIONS ON HOW TO WORK
THE WHEEL OF FORTUNE

First read through the List of Questions beginning on page x and choose a Question to which you sincerely desire an answer.

Concentrate your mind on the Question. Close your eyes and place your finger or a pointer on the Wheel of Fortune beneath:

Then open your eyes and look at the Symbol you have touched.

The next stage is best explained by giving you a couple of examples. Let us suppose that the question of your choice was Question 33: "Shall I prosper in my present venture?" And let us further suppose that when your eyes were closed your finger

or pointer touched the Symbol, or that segment of

the wheel containing the ☽ Symbol.

Turn to page xviii where you will find the figure 33, the number of your Question, in the column on the extreme left of the page headed "Number of Question". Follow the line of figures starting with 33 *across* the page towards the right until you arrive at the figure 68 which is contained in the column

headed by the ☽ Symbol.

This figure 68 is the number of the page where the answer to your Question will be found. Simply turn to page 68 and there,

opposite the ☽ Symbol, is your answer: "Yes, if you

change your present policy to some extent."

Here is another example. Let us suppose that you are seeking an answer to Question 47: "Shall I receive the offer I am hoping

for?"—and that your finger or pointer touched the

Symbol.

Turn to page xx where you will find the figure 47 in the extreme left hand column headed "Number of Question". Follow the line of figures starting with 47 across the page to the right until you arrive at the figure 20 contained in the column headed by

the Symbol. On page 20 you will find the answer

to your question opposite the Symbol: "Before

you do, you may receive a better one."

With every question you ask, and with each Symbol you touch in connection with it, use the same method. In every case, providing you ask a suitable question, and concentrate your mind on it during the working of the Wheel, the Oracle of the Wheel will give your answer to you with uncanny accuracy. Remember always that it is your concentrated thought which powers the Wheel.

If you ask a silly question—for example, Question 37: "Shall I ever have a home of my own?" at a time when in fact you *are* living in a home of your own, you will get a completely irrelevant answer—the Oracle's way of repaying attempted trickery.

In this, as in all things above and below, timing is important. There is a time to work the Wheel, and a time to put it aside. If your finger or pointer touches a spot *outside* the rim of the Wheel, or one of the spokes of the Wheel, this is a sign that you should put the Wheel aside for a day, then ask again. Never ask the same question twice on the same day.

It is not good to work the Wheel during the Dark of the Moon, that is, during the four days preceding the New Moon. The Dark of the Moon, for reasons which it is not possible to explain here, is not suitable for magical work of an active nature.

By timing your Questions correctly you will get the best results, for by doing so you will be swimming with, and not against, the Tides of Fortune.

QUESTIONS

1. Will my present situation soon be altered?
2. Shall I ever be rich?
3. Why have I not had a 'phone-call from . . , , .?
4. Should I emigrate?
5. Shall I soon be engaged to be married?
6. When shall I receive the news I am expecting?
7. Will my secret be discovered?
8. What does the man that I love think of me?
9. What does the woman that I love think of me?
10. How long will my present run of bad luck last?
11. Should I insist on a full explanation from . . . . .?
12. Will my dearest wish be granted?
13. Should I go ahead with the plan I have in mind?
14. What is the one that I care for thinking about at this moment?
15. Is there any real foundation for this fear that I have?
16. Should I forgive . . . . .?
17. What can I do to make my future successful?
18. How can I help with my friend's problem?
19. Am I ever likely to be involved in legal proceedings?
20. How can I win the love that I desire?
21. Is there any long-distance travel ahead for me?
22. Have I any enemies?
23. Will the person that I am thinking of return soon?
24. Will my life be adventurous?
25. Should I believe the promises made to me by . . . . .?
26. What will be the outcome of my present problems?
27. Will my health always be good?
28. Should I go into partnership with . . . . .?
29. Will my friends be happy to hear of my engagement?
30. Should I oppose . . . . .'s plan?
31. How should I answer this letter?
32. Shall I ever be free from this heartache and grief?
33. Shall I prosper in my present venture?
34. Of the two persons I am thinking of, which should I prefer?
35. What do people think of me?
36. What will happen at my appointed meeting with . . . . .?
37. Shall I ever have a home of my own?
38. Have I any rivals?
39. Shall I marry . . . . .?
40. Shall I move to a new address soon?
41. Should I accept the offer that has been made to me?

42. What can I do to please . . . . .?
43. Shall I cease to be a virgin before I marry?
44. Why have I not had a letter from . . . . .?
45. Ought I to give that which is asked of me?
46. Should I live in the country or town?
47. Shall I receive the offer I am hoping for?
48. Is my friend . . . . . to be trusted?
49. Shall I ever be famous?
50. Does . . . . . always tell me the truth?
51. Shall I have any children?
52. Shall I ever have my heart's desire?
53. Should I confess all to . . . . .?
54. Would I be more successful at home or abroad?
55. Shall I marry young?
56. Should I follow the advice given me by . . . . .?
57. How many lovers shall I have?
58. Shall I make a wealthy marriage?
59. Should I believe what . . . . . tells me?
60. Should I break it off or surrender?
61. What will happen if I do as . . . . . suggests?
62. Should I employ . . . . .?
63. How can I cope with . . . . . who is very temperamental and self-centred?
64. Shall I be happy in love?
65. Should I make the first move towards a reconciliation?
66. Shall I ever possess any property?
67. Shall I marry someone I already know?
68. What is the reason for the coolness between . . . . . and myself?
69. Am I expending my energies in the right direction?
70. Can I believe . . . . .'s encouraging words and praises?
71. What have I to expect in the immediate future?
72. Shall I ever get to know the person who attracts me so much?
73. Shall I ever know the truth about . . . . .?
74. What have I to expect between now and my next birthday?
75. Will the affair that I am now involved in last long?
76. Shall I fall in love again?
77. How long will the quarrel between . . . . . and myself last?
78. Is . . . . . faithful to me?
79. Should I tell my friend the truth about . . . . .?
80. Shall I achieve my main ambition in life?
81. What has happened to the thing that I have lost?
82. Can you give me some information about my future wife?
83. Can you give me some information about my future husband?
84. Should I change my job?
85. Am I right in my suspicions about . . . . .?
86. Shall I be lucky in my business affairs?

87. What is the cause of . . . . .'s animosity?
88. Where should I live when I retire?
89. Will my intended speculation prove fortunate?
90. Shall I marry again?
91. Should I stay with . . . . .?
92. In what occupation am I most likely to succeed?
93. Shall I be happy with . . . . .?
94. Will this connection that I have formed be a lasting one?
95. Has someone tried to create a rift between . . . . . and myself?
96. Will my life be peaceful or stormy?
97. Shall I be happy and prosperous in my old age?

TABLES

Number of Question ↓	⊙	☽	⛤	⚸	∞	𓂀	⛢
1	29	36	43	50	57	64	71
2	30	37	44	51	58	65	72
3	31	38	45	52	59	66	73
4	32	39	46	53	60	67	74
5	33	40	47	54	61	68	75
6	34	41	48	55	62	69	76
7	35	42	49	56	63	70	77
8	36	43	50	57	64	71	78
9	37	44	51	58	65	72	79
10	38	45	52	59	66	73	80
11	39	46	53	60	67	74	81
12	40	47	54	61	68	75	82

⚓	♋	⧖	☥	♉	☘	☯	⚲
78	85	92	2	9	16	23	30
79	86	93	3	10	17	24	31
80	87	94	4	11	18	25	32
81	88	95	5	12	19	26	33
82	89	96	6	13	20	27	34
83	90	97	7	14	21	28	35
84	91	1	8	15	22	29	36
85	92	2	9	16	23	30	37
86	93	3	10	17	24	31	38
87	94	4	11	18	25	32	39
88	95	5	12	19	26	33	40
89	96	6	13	20	27	34	41

Number of Question ↓	⊙	☽	✶	☦	∞	𓂀	⩜
13	41	48	55	62	69	76	83
14	42	49	56	63	70	77	84
15	43	50	57	64	71	78	85
16	44	51	58	65	72	79	86
17	45	52	59	66	73	80	87
18	46	53	60	67	74	81	88
19	47	54	61	68	75	82	89
20	48	55	62	69	76	83	90
21	49	56	63	70	77	84	91
22	50	57	64	71	78	85	92
23	51	58	65	72	79	86	93
24	52	59	66	73	80	87	94

⚓	♧	⧖	☥	♉	⚛	☯	⚢
90	97	7	14	21	28	35	42
91	1	8	15	22	29	36	43
92	2	9	16	23	30	37	44
93	3	10	17	24	31	38	45
94	4	11	18	25	32	39	46
95	5	12	19	26	33	40	47
96	6	13	20	27	34	41	48
97	7	14	21	28	35	42	49
1	8	15	22	29	36	43	50
2	9	16	23	30	37	44	51
3	10	17	24	31	38	45	52
4	11	18	25	32	39	46	53

Number of Question ↓	⊙	☽	⛤	✠	∞	𓂀	⧖
25	53	60	67	74	81	88	95
26	54	61	68	75	82	89	96
27	55	62	69	76	83	90	97
28	56	63	70	77	84	91	1
29	57	64	71	78	85	92	2
30	58	65	72	79	86	93	3
31	59	66	73	80	87	94	4
32	60	67	74	81	88	95	5
33	61	68	75	82	89	96	6
34	62	69	76	83	90	97	7
35	63	70	77	84	91	1	8
36	64	71	78	85	92	2	9

⚓	♣	⊠	☥	♉	△	☯	♀
5	12	19	26	33	40	47	54
6	13	20	27	34	41	48	55
7	14	21	28	35	42	49	56
8	15	22	29	36	43	50	57
9	16	23	30	37	44	51	58
10	17	24	31	38	45	52	59
11	18	25	32	39	46	53	60
12	19	26	33	40	47	54	61
13	20	27	34	41	48	55	62
14	21	28	35	42	49	56	63
15	22	29	36	43	50	57	64
16	23	30	37	44	51	58	65

Number of Question ↓	☉	☽	✪	⚘	∞	𓂀	Ⅹ
37	65	72	79	86	93	3	10
38	66	73	80	87	94	4	11
39	67	74	81	88	95	5	12
40	68	75	82	89	96	6	13
41	69	76	83	90	97	7	14
42	70	77	84	91	1	8	15
43	71	78	85	92	2	9	16
44	72	79	86	93	3	10	17
45	73	80	87	94	4	11	18
46	74	81	88	95	5	12	19
47	75	82	89	96	6	13	20
48	76	83	90	97	7	14	21

⚓	☘	⋈	☥	♉	△	☯	♀
17	24	31	38	45	52	59	66
18	25	32	39	46	53	60	67
19	26	33	40	47	54	61	68
20	27	34	41	48	55	62	69
21	28	35	42	49	56	63	70
22	29	36	43	50	57	64	71
23	30	37	44	51	58	65	72
24	31	38	45	52	59	66	73
25	32	39	46	53	60	67	74
26	33	40	47	54	61	68	75
27	34	41	48	55	62	69	76
28	35	42	49	56	63	70	77

Number of Question ↓	☉	☽	✶	☦	∞	𓂀	⚸
49	77	84	91	1	8	15	22
50	78	85	92	2	9	16	23
51	79	86	93	3	10	17	24
52	80	87	94	4	11	18	25
53	81	88	95	5	12	19	26
54	82	89	96	6	13	20	27
55	83	90	97	7	14	21	28
56	84	91	1	8	15	22	29
57	85	92	2	9	16	23	30
58	86	93	3	10	17	24	31
59	87	94	4	11	18	25	32
60	88	95	5	12	19	26	33

⚓	♋	⚔	☥	♉	⚛	☯	♀
29	36	43	50	57	64	71	78
30	37	44	51	58	65	72	79
31	38	45	52	59	66	73	80
32	39	46	53	60	67	74	81
33	40	47	54	61	68	75	82
34	41	48	55	62	69	76	83
35	42	49	56	63	70	77	84
36	43	50	57	64	71	78	85
37	44	51	58	65	72	79	86
38	45	52	59	66	73	80	87
39	46	53	60	67	74	81	88
40	47	54	61	68	75	82	89

Number of Question ↓	☉	☽	✶	☥	∞	𓂀	⟨
61	89	96	6	13	20	27	34
62	90	97	7	14	21	28	35
63	91	1	8	15	22	29	36
64	92	2	9	16	23	30	37
65	93	3	10	17	24	31	38
66	94	4	11	18	25	32	39
67	95	5	12	19	26	33	40
68	96	6	13	20	27	34	41
69	97	7	14	21	28	35	42
70	1	8	15	22	29	36	43
71	2	9	16	23	30	37	44
72	3	10	17	24	31	38	45

⚓	♧	⧖	♀	♉	☌	☯	♀
41	48	55	62	69	76	83	90
42	49	56	63	70	77	84	91
43	50	57	64	71	78	85	92
44	51	58	65	72	79	86	93
45	52	59	66	73	80	87	94
46	53	60	67	74	81	88	95
47	54	61	68	75	82	89	96
48	55	62	69	76	83	90	97
49	56	63	70	77	84	91	1
50	57	64	71	78	85	92	2
51	58	65	72	79	86	93	3
52	59	66	73	80	87	94	4

Number of Question ↓	☉	☽	✭	☿	∞	𓂀	⅄
73	4	11	18	25	32	39	46
74	5	12	19	26	33	40	47
75	6	13	20	27	34	41	48
76	7	14	21	28	35	42	49
77	8	15	22	29	36	43	50
78	9	16	23	30	37	44	51
79	10	17	24	31	38	45	52
80	11	18	25	32	39	46	53
81	12	19	26	33	40	47	54
82	13	20	27	34	41	48	55
83	14	21	28	35	42	49	56
84	15	22	29	36	43	50	57

☥	♧	⌧	☥	♉	⚶	☯	♀
53	60	67	74	81	88	95	5
54	61	68	75	82	89	96	6
55	62	69	76	83	90	97	7
56	63	70	77	84	91	1	8
57	64	71	78	85	92	2	9
58	65	72	79	86	93	3	10
59	66	73	80	87	94	4	11
60	67	74	81	88	95	5	12
61	68	75	82	89	96	6	13
62	69	76	83	90	97	7	14
63	70	77	84	91	1	8	15
64	71	78	85	92	2	9	16

Number of Question ↓	⊙	☽	☆	☖	∞	𓂀	Ⴟ
85	16	23	30	37	44	51	58
86	17	24	31	38	45	52	59
87	18	25	32	39	46	53	60
88	19	26	33	40	47	54	61
89	20	27	34	41	48	55	62
90	21	28	35	42	49	56	63
91	22	29	36	43	50	57	64
92	23	30	37	44	51	58	65
93	24	31	38	45	52	59	66
94	25	32	39	46	53	60	67
95	26	33	40	47	54	61	68
96	27	34	41	48	55	62	69
97	28	35	42	49	56	63	70

⚓	♋	✕	☤	♉	⚛	☯	⚥
65	72	79	86	93	3	10	17
66	73	80	87	94	4	11	18
67	74	81	88	95	5	12	19
68	75	82	89	96	6	13	20
69	76	83	90	97	7	14	21
70	77	84	91	1	8	15	22
71	78	85	92	2	9	16	23
72	79	86	93	3	10	17	24
73	80	87	94	4	11	18	25
74	81	88	95	5	12	19	26
75	82	89	96	6	13	20	27
76	83	90	97	7	14	21	28
77	84	91	1	8	15	22	29

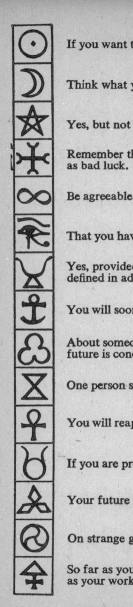

If you want to delude yourself, by all means.

Think what you like, but say little.

Yes, but not blindly.

Remember that too much good luck can be as bad as bad luck.

Be agreeable, amiable and devoted.

That you have great inner strength.

Yes, provided the areas of responsibility are clearly defined in advance.

You will soon be on your way.

About someone older, and influential so far as the future is concerned.

One person suspects, but will not speak of it.

You will reap the harvest of many well-spent years.

If you are prepared to travel.

Your future husband is now in a foreign country.

On strange ground.

So far as your private life is concerned, yes. So far as your work is concerned, definitely no.

1

A pleasant surprise.

Suck the honey, and ignore the thorns.

Not as many as you would like.

Well, nearly always.

This is entirely up to you.

It promises some good, some bad.

Happy and relieved.

Your worst enemy could be yourself.

You have nothing to fear in this respect.

He adores you madly—but he is changeable.

Not soon.

Give it another try.

It would be to your advantage to do so.

For a very brief space of time.

Yes.

2

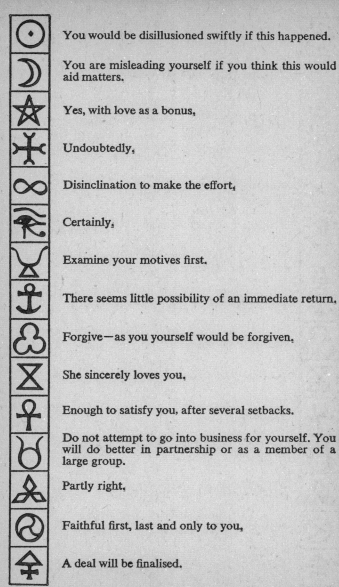

You would be disillusioned swiftly if this happened.

You are misleading yourself if you think this would aid matters.

Yes, with love as a bonus.

Undoubtedly.

Disinclination to make the effort.

Certainly.

Examine your motives first.

There seems little possibility of an immediate return.

Forgive—as you yourself would be forgiven.

She sincerely loves you.

Enough to satisfy you, after several setbacks.

Do not attempt to go into business for yourself. You will do better in partnership or as a member of a large group.

Partly right.

Faithful first, last and only to you.

A deal will be finalised.

3

Better let sleeping dogs lie.

Only through your own efforts.

Remember that two reports of the same thing are never exactly alike.

If you concentrate sufficiently hard on achieving it.

It may be wiser to refuse.

Yes.

Prudently. Do not put anything on paper that you might later regret.

If your desire is strong enough.

Opportunity often comes in disguise. Learn how to penetrate the veil.

Courage! It will not last forever.

There is no point in worrying about it. There are other fish in the sea.

Yes, if you are true.

Adopt a confident, positive, relaxed attitude and you cannot fail.

Not just yet.

There is no bar which cannot be overcome.

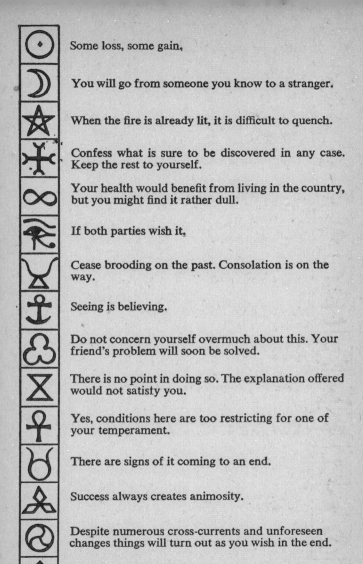

Some loss, some gain.

You will go from someone you know to a stranger.

When the fire is already lit, it is difficult to quench.

Confess what is sure to be discovered in any case. Keep the rest to yourself.

Your health would benefit from living in the country, but you might find it rather dull.

If both parties wish it.

Cease brooding on the past. Consolation is on the way.

Seeing is believing.

Do not concern yourself overmuch about this. Your friend's problem will soon be solved.

There is no point in doing so. The explanation offered would not satisfy you.

Yes, conditions here are too restricting for one of your temperament.

There are signs of it coming to an end.

Success always creates animosity.

Despite numerous cross-currents and unforeseen changes things will turn out as you wish in the end.

Not for a long, long time.

5

Perhaps longer than you wish.

A dislike of the company you keep.

Nothing very important.

Health and happiness at home. Fortune abroad.

You will lose nothing by waiting.

Not soon. When conditions have changed it will become possible.

You may go ahead with confidence.

You are not out of the woods yet, but the termination will be as you wish.

If you are, try to settle out of court.

You will be lucky.

This depends entirely on you.

No. The fault lies elsewhere.

Near woods, mountains, rivers, where there is plenty of room and fresh air.

You will soon be given a sign whereby you will know that you will recover it.

An uneventful interlude during which you will have time to formulate new plans.

6

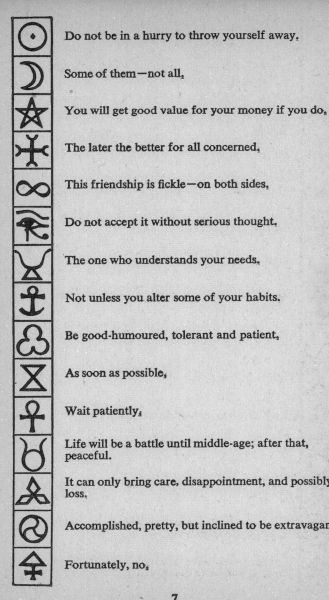

Do not be in a hurry to throw yourself away.

Some of them—not all.

You will get good value for your money if you do.

The later the better for all concerned.

This friendship is fickle—on both sides.

Do not accept it without serious thought.

The one who understands your needs.

Not unless you alter some of your habits.

Be good-humoured, tolerant and patient.

As soon as possible.

Wait patiently.

Life will be a battle until middle-age; after that, peaceful.

It can only bring care, disappointment, and possibly loss.

Accomplished, pretty, but inclined to be extravagant.

Fortunately, no.

7

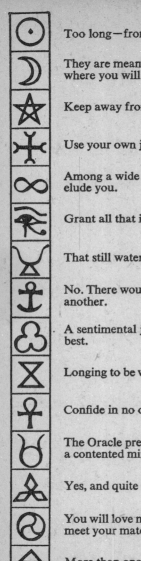

Too long—from your point of view.

They are meant to jockey you gently into a position where you will make a mistake.

Keep away from this person as much as possible.

Use your own judgement.

Among a wide circle of admirers. World fame may elude you.

Grant all that is asked.

That still waters run deep.

No. There would be one clash of temperament after another.

A sentimental journey will be the one you remember best.

Longing to be with you.

Confide in no one, and it will remain a secret.

The Oracle predicts a sufficiency for your needs and a contented mind.

Yes, and quite soon.

You will love many and deceive a few, but will finally meet your match in wedlock.

More than once.

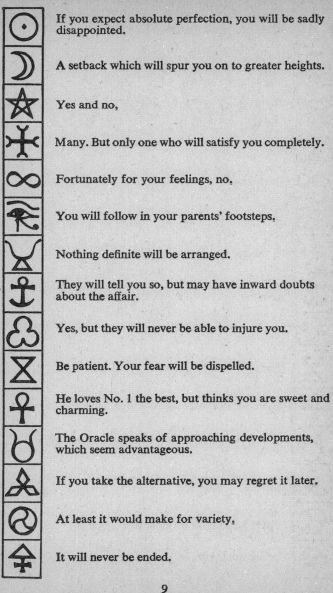	If you expect absolute perfection, you will be sadly disappointed.
	A setback which will spur you on to greater heights.
	Yes and no.
	Many. But only one who will satisfy you completely.
	Fortunately for your feelings, no.
	You will follow in your parents' footsteps.
	Nothing definite will be arranged.
	They will tell you so, but may have inward doubts about the affair.
	Yes, but they will never be able to injure you.
	Be patient. Your fear will be dispelled.
	He loves No. 1 the best, but thinks you are sweet and charming.
	The Oracle speaks of approaching developments, which seem advantageous.
	If you take the alternative, you may regret it later.
	At least it would make for variety.
	It will never be ended.

9

Why not? It can do no harm.

Highly improbable, in the sense that you mean.

A little delay will do no damage. Wait.

No, though you may have the opportunity.

It seems unlikely at the moment.

Lack of interest.

There are a few obstacles to be cleared first.

Opposition might do more harm than good.

Yes.

You should already have done so for your own peace of mind.

That you are ambitious.

Not as rich as you merit.

The seeker is an adept, and will prosper in almost any occupation.

Time will tell. Meanwhile, say nothing.

To some extent; not completely perhaps.

10

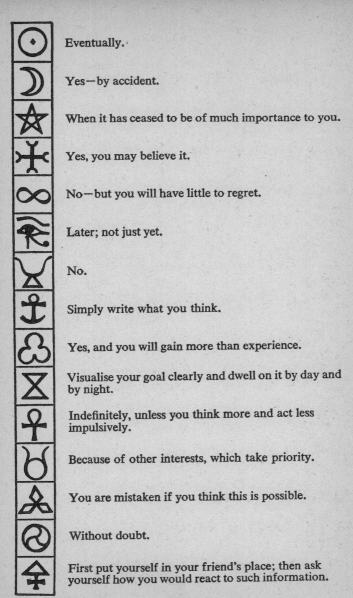

Eventually.

Yes—by accident.

When it has ceased to be of much importance to you.

Yes, you may believe it.

No—but you will have little to regret.

Later; not just yet.

No.

Simply write what you think.

Yes, and you will gain more than experience.

Visualise your goal clearly and dwell on it by day and by night.

Indefinitely, unless you think more and act less impulsively.

Because of other interests, which take priority.

You are mistaken if you think this is possible.

Without doubt.

First put yourself in your friend's place; then ask yourself how you would react to such information.

The loss is small in comparison with what you will soon gain.

A change of direction in your life, which will bring happiness.

The one destined for you is now in a far country.

Let your heart be your only guide.

Be completely honest. It is the only way.

Combine town life with weekends in the country if you can.

A newcomer, destined to play an important role in your future, may prevent this.

Sunlight breaks through the darkest clouds. Before long the world will seem a brighter place to you.

Certainly.

You cannot do much at the moment except assure your friend of your regard and willingness to help in any way possible.

It is the only way you will get to the heart of the matter.

Yes.

The link is strong and enduring.

Have you yourself been somewhat thoughtless or high-handed?

You will change your ideas about your main ambition within the next three years. Then ask again.

Outspoken, rather quick-tempered. Has a strange accent.

Longer than it has already lasted.

A feeling of inadequacy.

It will mark the start of a lucky phase in your life.

You will flourish in a far-off country.

Do not wait for it. You will be better off without it.

Yes.

Money is needed to ensure success.

You will live through them, and find contentment.

If you have been in the past, you will again.

Not completely.

To some extent circumstances are against it; yet it may happen.

Yes, and succeeded.

In a non-hilly region, within reach of the sea.

A greater treausre than that which you have lost will be found during your search.

13

You are too romantic. Think in more practical terms before you marry or your happiness will be brief.

The later, the better.

You could not expend them in any other direction at present.

Another would be more suitable for your needs.

Young in years, old in experience.

This person has an axe to grind; but is also fond of you.

Yes, if it pleases you.

Value both.

You will live to a ripe old age, with all your faculties intact.

By appearing less eager.

Wait a little.

At any moment.

Peaceful, on the whole.

After a slow and tedious start, you will prosper.

You will marry a woman who will make your life comfortable and happy.

14

Certainly there are others in which you would do equally well.

The shorter the better, for all concerned.

They are as sincere as they can be.

If you want peace at any price, agree with whatever this person says or does. If you are prepared for a battle, take a strong line.

You are in danger of being misled.

The harder you work, the luckier you will be.

Make more effort.

You are better liked than you think.

It would be tough going at first, but could lead to fortune.

Yes. The longest way round will be the shortest way home for you.

Of an interesting offer.

By the time it is known, circumstances will have changed.

Yes, if you are wise and make provision for it now.

Weigh up the advantages offered before taking this step.

An affectionate man, who will be the comfort of your life and the staff of your old age.

This may always be a mystery to you.

Unfaithful in the past, but may be true in the future.

A gift, a 'phone-call and an invitation.

You will find more pleasure than pain.

Only the first and the last love will linger in your mind.

When it suits the occasion.

Yes, but it will be a matter of little consequence.

It will be followed by a more eventful one.

Happier than some of your relatives.

If your friends are few, you wil have fewer enemies.

It is wise to be cautious.

His thoughts veer in many directions.

Yes.

On a long-term basis, it will be better for you to stay.

It is not advisable at this stage.

16

Yes, considerable increase is indicated.

Discretion is the best policy.

If you go the right way about it.

No.

Wealthy but brief.

Yes; one of them will have a special talent.

News is on its way.

But for an error of judgement in the past, you would be living in it now.

Do not interfere unless you must.

Turn your thoughts in another direction.

Yes.

That you have a certain charm.

The Oracle does not promise great wealth, but you will be more fortunate than many.

Anything which includes a lively, varied schedule and does not involve close supervision.

You are attaching too much importance to this.

You stand in the way.

Yes.

You would not like it.

Yes. Luck will play a part in this.

Some of it; not all by a long chalk.

What you are hoping for at present will not happen. Something better will.

You have given so much in the past; why not now?

Several, but you have a charmed life.

Say little and write even less is always a safe policy.

Wait and see.

Plan slowly; act quickly.

Changes difficult to effect, delays, complications on all sides; nevertheless you will win through in the end.

It will soon arrive, and you will be told the reason for the delay.

Happier than you have ever been before.

If you can learn the gentle art of co-operation.

18

In an old house, in the country.

Whatever you have lost will be found, but not for a while.

You will make new contacts, one at least of which will be valuable to you.

Yes. You spoke together recently.

With a bit of delicate manoeuvring, you may be able to arrive at a compromise.

Yes; you will be forgiven.

Remain where you are for the present, at any rate.

It will be your passport to fulfillment.

Your outlook will be completely altered by a strange twist of Destiny.

Yes, if you act fairly.

Without breaking any confidences, discuss this affair with someone who is experienced in such problems; then act.

Insist, and keep on insisting until you get it.

No.

A chain is as strong as its weakest link.

Lack of attention and appreciation on your part.

19

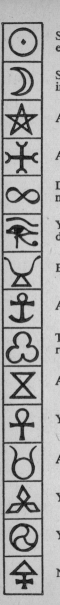

Some hindrances at first, but the omens are good for eventual success.

She has a good figure, and a small, independent income.

As long as you want it to last.

Another claim.

Do not act on this suggestion immediately. Give it more thought.

Your talents will find a profitable outlet some distance from your home.

Before you do, you may receive a better one.

Anything you tackle now is likely to succeed.

To some degree; your next venture will be more rewarding.

A new approach to these problems will solve them.

Yes; but this will simply be a vexation, not a tragedy.

At a time when you least expect it.

You will have more than one opportunity.

Yes; someone who is envious of you.

Not too near and not too far from your relatives.

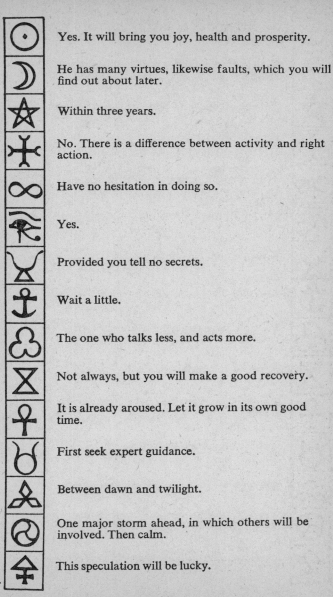

Yes. It will bring you joy, health and prosperity.

He has many virtues, likewise faults, which you will find out about later.

Within three years.

No. There is a difference between activity and right action.

Have no hesitation in doing so.

Yes.

Provided you tell no secrets.

Wait a little.

The one who talks less, and acts more.

Not always, but you will make a good recovery.

It is already aroused. Let it grow in its own good time.

First seek expert guidance.

Between dawn and twilight.

One major storm ahead, in which others will be involved. Then calm.

This speculation will be lucky.

21

If you can put up with certain things, it will work out to your advantage in the long run.

Yes; it should not be too difficult for you to find a more congenial atmosphere.

If it ended today, it could begin again tomorrow.

Believe them. They are sincere.

If you are in an independent position, have nothing to do with this person. If you are not, only patience and diplomacy will answer the case.

No.

Yes, overnight.

Try, or at least appear, to be more detached.

You are greatly loved.

You will gain nothing by it.

You will travel to one of the greatest cities in the world.

About various tasks which must be done.

Do not fret. Your secret is secure.

You will have respect, congenial company and no financial worries.

Much depends on your own attitude.

In one where your exceptional powers of organisation can be put to good use.

Absolutely right.

You are deceiving yourself if you think so.

Developments which could have an important bearing on your future.

In your fashion.

Not as many as you could have, for not everyone pleases you.

Yes; you can depend on this.

Experience can be a great asset in any new venture.

You will get a surprise.

There will be more congratulations than criticism.

Your greatest enemy will be rendered powerless.

You are worrying yourself needlessly.

That you may deceive him.

There will soon be cause for rejoicing.

No.

Enjoy it while it lasts.

Success is within your grasp.

Your friend is entitled to know.

Let it happen without making any apparent effort.

At least let it be known that you harbour no ill-feeling.

You may have to choose between money and love.

The choice will be yours.

Preoccupation with other interests and affairs.

In the not too distant future.

Do all in your power to oppose this plan.

The chances seem better now than they have been for some time.

There is no point in not doing so.

She thinks well of you . . . at the moment.

Marriage may bring you wealth.

Whatever occupation you follow, you will eclipse your contemporaries, outlive your relatives and die rich.

This will depend very much on how you behave.

Simply envy.

No.

Some of it.

Yes—in return for past kindness.

Make a few inquiries first.

Not if one person, at least, can frustrate you in this.

It is time to take a firm line, and say no.

One that you think of as a friend.

As your intuition dictates.

For a time, after which you will be content to settle down.

Do not allow yourself to be distracted by trifles or time-wasters.

Not until you revise your ideas in some directions.

You may not like the explanation when you get it.

In many ways, yes.

No. You have not come up to expectations.

Avoid isolated surroundings, and proximity to water.

You will recover it in a most surprising fashion.

Something you have been longing for is sure to happen.

There will be a choice between someone you know and a newcomer.

Surrender could be sweet.

Think well how it would affect everyone before you do so.

Town life confines your spirit. A country place would suit you better.

Perhaps, after a time.

Devote thought, energy and time to helping others —and you, also, will be helped.

Do not be too trusting.

Very soon, you will have a flash of inspiration about this. Act on it.

A vital fact will be kept back if you do.

The spirit of adventure should not be quenched.

Yes.

More peaceful than it has been.

Yes; then be on your guard against those who would like to relieve you of the proceeds.

Very intelligent, although she has not had much formal education; passionate.

The longer, the better.

There is no coolness—on the contrary. Circumstances intervene.

It is not in your best interests to act on this suggestion.

When an opportunity to go abroad comes up, take it.

There may be a change of mind about this.

More than likely.

The path is rugged, but you will reach the peaks.

Changes are about to take place which will ease your mind.

There may be threats, but no legal proceedings.

Yes.

No—luckily for you.

Only yourself.

You will be content.

It would be better for you if you did.

You will meet him on holiday, or a business trip.

It is not too late.

Only to a very minor degree.

Yes.

Not very. You seek for the ideal match—which is a time-absorbing task.

In some matters, yes.

Not if it will affect a relationship with someone who is important to you.

Both have a sincere regard for you.

Only minor ailments will afflict you.

By changing some of your habits.

Caution is required.

Sooner than you think.

When all inner and outer conflicts have been resolved, then and only then can you expect peace.

28

It may be worse before it is better.

No.

Yes, if you want more money.

The other party must make the first move.

Not all of them.

There is a good as well as a bad side to this person. Try harder to bring out the good side.

It may not be in your best interests to follow it.

Later on perhaps; not soon.

Why attempt the impossible?

You baffle them a bit at times by your behaviour.

If you have any doubts, do not let yourself be persuaded into this.

Fate decrees that you will travel far.

About something you said.

This depends upon one act of yours.

You will have more happiness and better fortune in your old age than in your youth.

No, but don't despair.

Work which brings you in contact with the public.

No. Put them out of your mind.

Faithful one day; inconstant the next.

You will explore new territory, and find congenial company.

If you can put the wishes of another before your own.

More than one.

You sometimes make this very difficult by your own attitude.

Yes.

It will mark the start of a more satisfying chapter in your life.

More surprised than happy.

Success will inevitably create enmity in certain quarters.

Consult someone who is qualified to advise you in this area.

He admires you.

Much thought and a stroke of luck are required before a change sets in.

If you never get one, so much the better for you.

For a brief spell.

Prosperity is knocking at your door, but someone seems reluctant to open it. Yourself, perhaps?

Emphatically, no.

By subtle strategy, yes. Anything blatant would be off-putting.

Certainly, if you wish to be quickly reconciled.

Wealth comes after a few years of struggle.

At least one who will be a great comfort to you.

Responsibilities and work intervene.

Someone who thinks well of you will give you the key.

Opposition might cost you dear.

There will be a decision to make before this can happen.

Yes—but try to make sure that the same situation does not recur.

That you mean more than you say.

Look forward to a windfall from an unexpected source.

31

You might lose more than you gain if you do.

You may be the one to break it.

A remark which you thought would not be repeated.

Good luck combined with good guidance and enterprise will guarantee this.

Do not dwell on the subject. It is a waste of precious you.

Do not depend on it.

Why not? It is the truth.

You certainly deserve it, but may have to be satisfied with an alternative.

Yes.

None that matter.

Do not be in too great a hurry. You have yet to make up your mind about a few important points.

Yes, whether you like it or not.

Learn to work with others, and when the time comes, to delegate to others.

When you realise that it is mostly of your own making, and do something about it, your luck will improve.

For the reason which you suspect.

32

Not if a third party can prevent it.

You cannot please all of the people all of the time.

Back to your birth-place, if possible.

By offering a small reward, it will quickly be restored to you.

Improvement in certain matters and a disappointment from which you will recover.

Yes, if you keep on as you are doing.

If you want to do the sensible thing, break it off. Surrender if you want short-term happiness.

Silence is golden in this case.

You should live high up, in a house with plenty of light, near the sea.

You might live to repent it if you do.

In less than a twelvemonth you will be cheerful again. Meanwhile, make the most of the assets you have.

Yes.

This is a Karmic lesson which your friend must learn.

You would do better to wait until an explanation is offered without any pressure from you.

You should always take your wares to the best market, however far-off it may be.

33

There are signs of some confusion and delay in the matter.

Both.

Do not be over-confident about this; the outcome is doubtful.

Good-natured, good-looking, fond of the good things in life.

It will develop into a closer link.

Another person's jealousy.

You know from your own experience what will happen.

By leaving your native land you will gain knowledge, honours and wealth.

Certainly. Quite quickly.

It will all be settled, without much effort on your part.

Warning! You have rivals to contend with.

Be confident; the chances are in your favour.

It is possible.

No—which will turn out to be a blessing in disguise.

Not soon; you are somewhat fastidious.

34

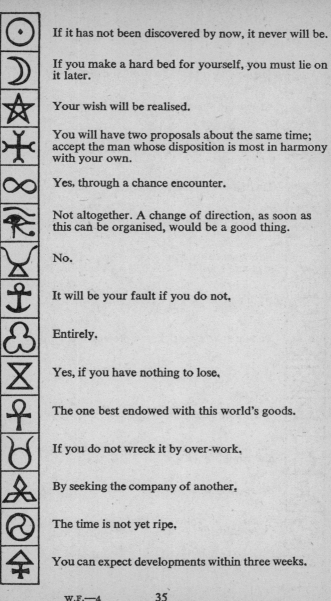

If it has not been discovered by now, it never will be.

If you make a hard bed for yourself, you must lie on it later.

Your wish will be realised.

You will have two proposals about the same time; accept the man whose disposition is most in harmony with your own.

Yes, through a chance encounter.

Not altogether. A change of direction, as soon as this can be organised, would be a good thing.

No.

It will be your fault if you do not.

Entirely.

Yes, if you have nothing to lose.

The one best endowed with this world's goods.

If you do not wreck it by over-work.

By seeking the company of another.

The time is not yet ripe.

You can expect developments within three weeks.

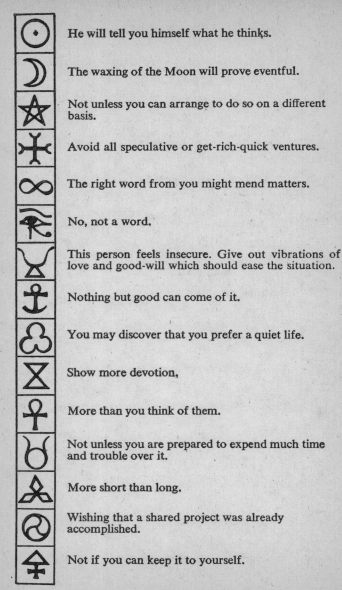

He will tell you himself what he thinks.

The waxing of the Moon will prove eventful.

Not unless you can arrange to do so on a different basis.

Avoid all speculative or get-rich-quick ventures.

The right word from you might mend matters.

No, not a word.

This person feels insecure. Give out vibrations of love and good-will which should ease the situation.

Nothing but good can come of it.

You may discover that you prefer a quiet life.

Show more devotion.

More than you think of them.

Not unless you are prepared to expend much time and trouble over it.

More short than long.

Wishing that a shared project was already accomplished.

Not if you can keep it to yourself.

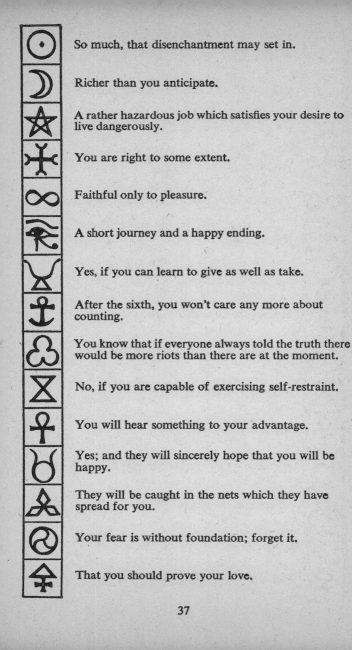

So much, that disenchantment may set in.

Richer than you anticipate.

A rather hazardous job which satisfies your desire to live dangerously.

You are right to some extent.

Faithful only to pleasure.

A short journey and a happy ending.

Yes, if you can learn to give as well as take.

After the sixth, you won't care any more about counting.

You know that if everyone always told the truth there would be more riots than there are at the moment.

No, if you are capable of exercising self-restraint.

You will hear something to your advantage.

Yes; and they will sincerely hope that you will be happy.

They will be caught in the nets which they have spread for you.

Your fear is without foundation; forget it.

That you should prove your love.

37

It is almost over.

This call will come when you have almost ceased to think about it.

There seems very little chance of this, unless you are prepared to be a door-mat.

Despite many restrictions and hard knocks you will be, eventually.

If you do, there may be unexpected repercussions.

Should this happen, you will only be one of many.

Do what you know is right.

There will be a sufficiency for your needs.

Yes, your own, and possibly another's.

You will not hear until a choice or decision has been made.

Sooner than you anticipate.

If you do, you may not like the consequences.

The later the better for you.

What have you to gain by harbouring ill-will?

That your standards are high.

38

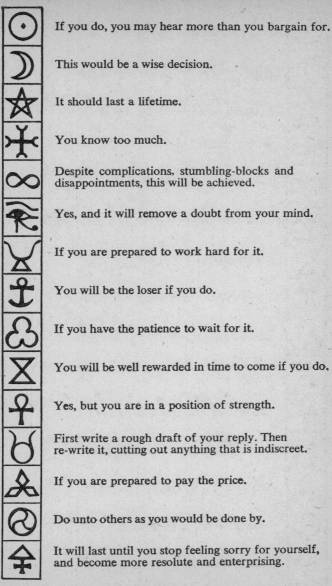

If you do, you may hear more than you bargain for.

This would be a wise decision.

It should last a lifetime.

You know too much.

Despite complications, stumbling-blocks and disappointments, this will be achieved.

Yes, and it will remove a doubt from your mind.

If you are prepared to work hard for it.

You will be the loser if you do.

If you have the patience to wait for it.

You will be well rewarded in time to come if you do.

Yes, but you are in a position of strength.

First write a rough draft of your reply. Then re-write it, cutting out anything that is indiscreet.

If you are prepared to pay the price.

Do unto others as you would be done by.

It will last until you stop feeling sorry for yourself, and become more resolute and enterprising.

No; but there is something better in store for you.

It is possible, but not quite definite.

No. It is simply a misunderstanding which can soon be sorted out.

Within fifty miles of your present home.

It will be recovered by chance.

Enlightenment. A new sense of values. Travel.

No.

It may already be too late to break it off.

By doing so, you will ease your own mind at another's expense.

You should go South, to a country place, near a river or lake.

Where you now look for happiness you may not find it, but everything comes to those who wait.

Yes; if you can open your mind to new possibilities. There is someone who can console you.

Not until proof is forthcoming.

Do not offer help unless you are asked for it.

This would be useless; but you may get it from another quarter.

No. Abandon it.

The Oracle speaks clearly of a speedy arrival.

You would find a completely peaceful existence very dull.

This speculation comes under fickle fortune, but your next one will be rewarding.

Not so much beautiful as attractive. A pleasing personality. Reasonably domesticated.

If you so desire.

An unfounded rumour.

Do what you think is right.

Travel will prove beneficial to you and yours.

Possibly, but it would be a mistake to build your hopes too high.

Before very long, you will be inviting your friends to a house-warming party.

If you are careful about signing a document.

Persevere. Fortune will crown your efforts.

Yes, but the settlement will be in your favour.

Not for some time.

41

Of last night's dream.

A secret shared by two is no secret.

If you act with due care and forethought now.

Later; there is an obstacle in the way at present.

The one you are thinking of now would bring you grief. Look around and you will find a more desirable partner than your present favourite.

This could happen, if you vary your usual routine.

So far as your work is concerned, yes. So far as your leisure is concerned, no.

If you want someone who is dependable and reliable, by all means.

The proper time will be when you have learned to distinguish between tinsel and gold.

Ask around, and you will find out.

Examine it carefully first for any hidden drawbacks.

The one you see first.

If you pay more attention to diet and leisure.

You have it, but the path is not yet clear.

Another and better one will soon be devised.

42

Time will banish this fear.

That you will do.

To some extent, yes.

You would be better off elsewhere.

Think well before you make a switch, as a change for the better is indicated in your present occupation.

Long enough for a reconciliation to be a heartfelt relief.

They are both sincere and well-merited.

Put as great a distance as possible between this person and yourself.

This advice is well-meant, but worthless.

The price may be too high.

Before long, you will be less concerned about this.

That you could be more forthcoming.

You have already surmised what will happen if you do, and you are right.

A journey of a million miles begins with a single step.

About the past, with some regrets.

43

Forgive *and* forget.

That you are inclined to be too demanding at times.

A rich harvest will benefit you.

Ideally, you should have been trained for it since childhood. Now your best chances lie in a Government or Civil Service post.

You can decide this when you are in possession of the full facts; not before.

True as steel, but do not over-tax this devotion.

Money will slip through your fingers.

Unalloyed bliss would bore you.

One who will more than make up for any previous disappointments.

Always, when you can check up on it.

Long before.

If you do not exercise self-control, the consequences could be unfortunate.

Some of them will hope that it will be broken off.

A powerful friend will counteract the malice of your foes.

You will realise the truth when you have discussed your fear with an experienced person.

44

Find out what is needed. Then supply it.

It is the forerunner of a long cycle of good luck.

For a very good reason, which you may never be told.

Yes, this is a true affinity.

If you choose your associates carefully.

Your friends may already know.

If you did, your feelings would not be returned.

Do you want to court more humiliation?

It is your best chance of happiness.

Yes, but they may not be your own.

You are not forgotten; be patient.

Yes, and you will be very proud of it.

No.

Do not expect any definite news as yet.

It is not like you to be unkind.

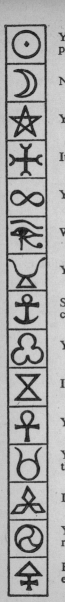

You will help most by being there when your presence is needed.

No.

You are being wasted here. Why not?

It will last as long as you want it to last.

Your somewhat exacting standards.

When you aim for another goal.

Yes, but it will get you nowhere.

Someone of means is thinking of you in this connection.

Yes, completely.

It is yours—if you know how to go about it.

You will be asked for more if you do.

Yes; but they are more of an annoyance than a threat.

Ignore it.

Yes, and there will be a pot of gold at the end of the rainbow.

Build up good-will, and do your best to transform enemies into allies.

46

Only in a very minor way.

Within a twelve-month, if at all.

A third person has to be considered.

Neither you, nor a third person, has created this rift.

The simple life might prove too complicated for you. A garden-suburb with all modern amenities would be better.

It is not lost; it has only been too carefully laid aside.

Possibly a change of address. Joy from one source; sadness from another.

You will marry the one who wishes to marry you.

You know what is the right thing to do. But will you do it?

Better today than tomorrow.

Both suit you, one as well as the other.

No.

Quite soon, if you will concentrate on helping those who are carrying heavier burdens than your own.

Some of them.

Your friendship itself is a big help.

47

Make your own feelings clear.

The later the better.

It is on its way.

Admit you believe that a battle a day keeps boredom at bay.

Three times you will be in danger of losing, but the fourth time you will win.

She will be older than you, and will give you security, comfort and warm affection.

The end is in sight.

Something was said which was never meant.

Something which will surprise you — pleasantly.

Your days will be lengthened if you move to a different climate.

You may have to wait what seems to you a very long time.

After some delay, help will come unexpectedly.

Yes, if you do not over-extend yourself.

Your losses will be small in comparison to your gains.

You know the policy you must pursue if you wish to avoid this happening.

Both long and short and fairly frequent.

Of your next meeting.

Sooner or later, but more good than bad will result.

Free from sorrow and financial pressures, as you deserve.

Not while you live under your present roof.

Your partner will be the handsomest man in the neighbourhood.

Not today, or tomorrow.

There should be a better balance between energy devoted to work and to play.

You could never be quite certain about this person's loyalty.

If you so desire.

Your friend is trusty and true.

Yes at once.

The younger one.

You have many healthy years ahead of you.

Be less available.

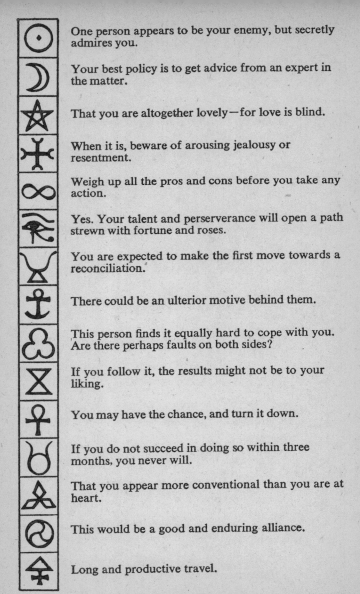 ☉	One person appears to be your enemy, but secretly admires you.
☽	Your best policy is to get advice from an expert in the matter.
⛤	That you are altogether lovely—for love is blind.
⸸	When it is, beware of arousing jealousy or resentment.
∞	Weigh up all the pros and cons before you take any action.
𓂀	Yes. Your talent and perserverance will open a path strewn with fortune and roses.
♉	You are expected to make the first move towards a reconciliation.
⚓	There could be an ulterior motive behind them.
⯒	This person finds it equally hard to cope with you. Are there perhaps faults on both sides?
⊠	If you follow it, the results might not be to your liking.
☥	You may have the chance, and turn it down.
♉	If you do not succeed in doing so within three months, you never will.
⚇	That you appear more conventional than you are at heart.
☯	This would be a good and enduring alliance.
⚯	Long and productive travel.

You will hear news about this in the near future.

Are you completely without fault?

That it may be hard to keep up with you.

Someone of whom you little think may be instrumental in improving your fortune.

The kind of job which gives you freedom to move around.

You will discover a very important clue very soon.

Always has been, always will be.

A gain, a loss, and a change of mind.

It is your reason for living.

More than one at a time to begin with.

Sometimes—when it slips out by accident.

Someone like you is bound to have many temptations.

In some strange way it will bring you luck.

A few consider you are acting rashly. Others admire your courage.

They may triumph for a season, but yours will be the final victory.

More by night than by day.

Always have two strings to your bow.

Seven more months.

You will get it soon, and all will be explained.

The joys will outnumber the sorrows.

If you channel your energies in the right direction, not otherwise.

First give the matter more thought.

It may happen, but is hardly likely to bring you joy.

Without delay.

Rich in love and contentment if not in worldly possessions.

Sooner or later.

When contact is made, it may be too late. Your interests will have veered in another direction.

Yes, through a series of developments of which you know little at present.

Discuss the matter further before making any firm decision about this.

It is doubtful.

No.

Simply by listening when your friend wants to talk about this problem.

If you insist, you will get an explanation of a sort— not necessarily the true one.

It is a case of "far-off hills look green". Better stay where you are.

It may last longer than you wish.

You are too popular.

You will be greatly helped by the good-will and co-operation of at least two people.

Not the whole truth.

It may come to you by chance, a lucky gamble or speculation.

If you are wise, you will believe it.

All it needs is courage and tenacity.

If you do not give, it may be taken from you.

There is one who is eager to take your place.

Don't answer it at all until you have shown it to a wiser and more experienced person whom you can trust.

Perhaps more than you bargain for.

Not the one which you dread.

Yes, but there will be no adverse publicity.

Yes. By which time, it will no longer be your heart's desire.

Too soon for some, too late for others.

Someone has tried to do so, but will not succeed for long.

There are three suitable alternatives; in a rural area, on the coast, or near a river.

Search diligently for it, and give up any suspicions of dishonesty.

Improvement in health. Fresh interests. Success of a plan.

You will be given a sign within the next three months.

If you surrender today, it may be broken off tomorrow.

A full confession might do more harm than good. Take the middle path.

In the country, inland, but not in a valley.

Yes.

Yes. You will emerge from the shadows a stronger and wiser personality.

Do not depend upon them.

54

Come now! Even Hercules must have had his off days.

This love cannot be won—it must be freely given.

You should have done so before now.

Enquire again in twenty-four hours.

You have too active a mind to lead an altogether peaceful life.

Avoid all speculations if possible now; within three months prospects brighten.

She will have a domineering disposition, but by your own methods you will get your own way in most things.

No, this cannot happen.

A preference for someone else.

Why should you hesitate? This is an excellent suggestion.

You will meet with many changes of fortune abroad.

Another one is on the way.

Someone you do not know at present will help to bring this about. Meanwhile, be patient.

Bend your efforts in another direction.

Important developments will shortly alter the situation.

There would be little profit, and much vexation.

Several trips, by land, sea and air.

Of cash which is needed, and how it can be acquired.

There is some risk of discovery, but this can be avoided.

More so, perhaps, than you merit.

Love is waiting for you.

You will be an old man's darling, not a young man's slave.

More deeply than before.

No; it was a mistake from the start, but can still be rectified.

You will make life easier for yourself if you do.

Curb your impatience. A good thing is worth waiting for.

No.

You deserve more than this.

The one whose background is similar to your own.

You will be healthy and vigorous to a good old age.

56

Your true friends, yes.

Someone you refused a favour is hostile to you.

It is an illusion. Banish it from your mind.

That you are faithful.

The same influences prevail for a time. Then there is hope.

Things can only worsen if you do.

Not until you have a firm and better offer.

If either side is obstinate, it could last forever.

Put your faith in deeds, not words.

When and only when you become completely detached, this person will no longer have any power to upset you.

You should follow this advice. But will you?

Not in your chosen field. Perhaps elsewhere.

You deserve appreciation from this quarter, but you may not get it.

That your bark is worse than your bite.

If you are prepared to take a chance, yes.

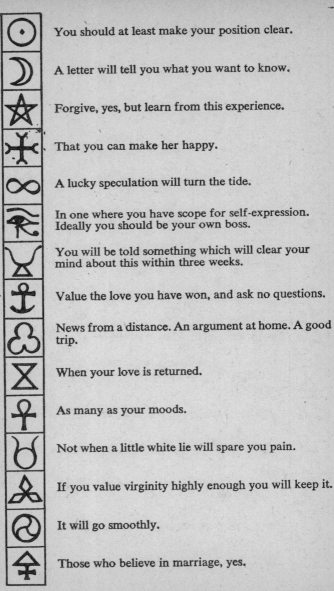	You should at least make your position clear.
	A letter will tell you what you want to know.
	Forgive, yes, but learn from this experience.
	That you can make her happy.
	A lucky speculation will turn the tide.
	In one where you have scope for self-expression. Ideally you should be your own boss.
	You will be told something which will clear your mind about this within three weeks.
	Value the love you have won, and ask no questions.
	News from a distance. An argument at home. A good trip.
	When your love is returned.
	As many as your moods.
	Not when a little white lie will spare you pain.
	If you value virginity highly enough you will keep it.
	It will go smoothly.
	Those who believe in marriage, yes.

Briefly, and to the point.

Why should you doubt it?

Perfect yourself in what you want to do—not what others think you should do.

It will change overnight; quickly.

Depend upon it, you are not forgotten. You will soon be in contact again.

Happiness lies ahead.

If you can recognise Lady Luck when you see her.

If this can be done without causing trouble.

Yes.

As you are in the wrong, it is up to you.

Yes, if you can.

Sooner than you plan, perhaps.

Another person intervenes.

Perhaps more than one.

If you disapprove of it, say so.

Yes; in less than half the time it has already lasted.

Why ask, when you know the answer already?

Sympathy is not enough. Give also whatever practical assistance you can.

If you can do so without getting over-emotional about it.

Yes, but not until you have done all the preliminary research thoroughly.

It will be brief.

You are regarded as a threat.

You are very ambitious. You will attempt and achieve great things.

Never.

Behind-the-scenes activities could play a part in this.

Sift out the wheat from the chaff.

When you have almost lost heart, not before.

If it will give you pleasure.

Not at the moment.

Do not delay. The sooner you answer it the sooner it will be off your mind.

60

You will be better off than before.

Loss in one direction, gain in another.

Not if you keep on the right side of the law.

When it comes within your grasp, you will be wishing for something else.

Sooner than you think.

Let the matter rest for the moment.

You should live in a house which catches all the sunlight, within easy reach of friends, neighbours and contacts.

A member of your family, or someone who lives under the same roof, will find it for you.

Many experiences, not all of them rewarding. Disharmony which is avoidable. An offer, which you should take.

Yes.

It is better to bend than to break.

You will gain nothing by concealing the truth.

If you wish for health, in the country; for wealth, in town.

It is your path to happiness.

It will be relieved sooner than you imagine.

Why choose? If possible, have both.

If you remember that even metal gets fatigued, and take enough rest.

You have already won it; but there are certain barriers.

It would be folly to hesitate.

Something hinders its arrival, but it will come.

If it is stormy, this will be of your own making.

Delay speculation for the moment if you would be successful.

She will be an orphan, with little money, but you will be spared in-law troubles.

It is nearly over.

You have been too outspoken.

This suggestion is well-meant, but think twice before adopting it.

If you set off on a lucky day, you will be successful.

When it arrives, you may be torn in two directions.

Yes, for a short time.

By proceeding cautiously you will prosper.

Opinions vary, depending on how well they know you.

Despite some differences in temperament, this would be a good partnership.

Long voyaging, and a safe return.

Only of you.

Not if you are discreet.

You will be solvent, and well cared for.

Do not make any change in your present status without careful thought.

If you can persuade him to change some of his habits, you will be content.

Very quickly.

You know you are not.

Yes; this person would be an asset in many ways.

Yes, if you are more concerned with love than money.

More so than you may imagine.

Refuse it.

The one with the lively mind.

Nothing that need worry you.

One of them will be sad.

Critics, yes—but no real enemies.

The truth will be revealed if you seek it from the right source.

That you bring out the best and the worst in him.

Sooner or later.

The next development will make your decision for you.

You know what you want. Keep trying for it.

If it lasts much longer, it may never be mended.

Yes. The one who uttered them is no idle flatterer.

This person is envious of you for a certain reason. Knowing this should make it easier for you to be tolerant.

This advice is good for the one who gave it, but not for you.

You are already quite well-known. Be satisfied.

This would require a minor miracle. Look elsewhere.

That you are impetuous.

64

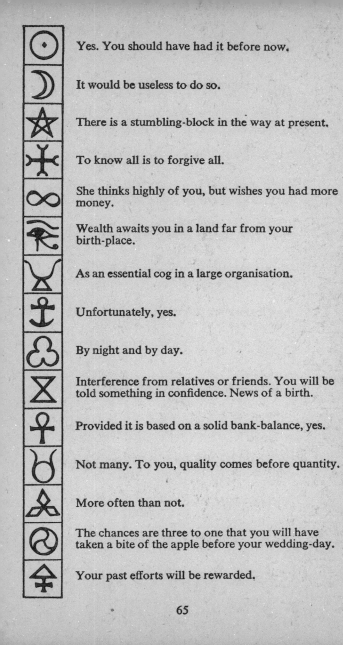

Yes. You should have had it before now.

It would be useless to do so.

There is a stumbling-block in the way at present.

To know all is to forgive all.

She thinks highly of you, but wishes you had more money.

Wealth awaits you in a land far from your birth-place.

As an essential cog in a large organisation.

Unfortunately, yes.

By night and by day.

Interference from relatives or friends. You will be told something in confidence. News of a birth.

Provided it is based on a solid bank-balance, yes.

Not many. To you, quality comes before quantity.

More often than not.

The chances are three to one that you will have taken a bite of the apple before your wedding-day.

Your past efforts will be rewarded.

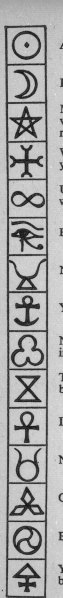

As many as you merit.

Do not answer it until you have had expert advice.

Many adventures ahead. Some you will have to be very discreet about; others you will be happy to recall.

With your personality and talent there is no need for you to ask such a question.

Unknown to you, things are already happening which will work out to your advantage.

Because the interest is one-sided.

Not unless you are prepared to play second fiddle.

Your personality will be the deciding factor in this.

Not necessary. Your friend already has more than an inkling.

This person is already aware of you. Let things blossom gradually.

If you do, the outcome may not please you.

No.

One by chance.

Because of a minor indisposition.

Your own efforts combined with a stroke of luck will bring this about.

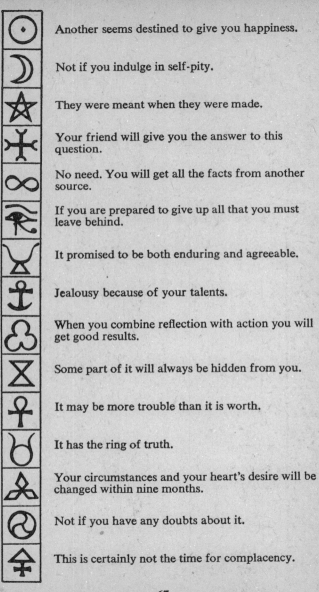

Another seems destined to give you happiness.

Not if you indulge in self-pity.

They were meant when they were made.

Your friend will give you the answer to this question.

No need. You will get all the facts from another source.

If you are prepared to give up all that you must leave behind.

It promised to be both enduring and agreeable.

Jealousy because of your talents.

When you combine reflection with action you will get good results.

Some part of it will always be hidden from you.

It may be more trouble than it is worth.

It has the ring of truth.

Your circumstances and your heart's desire will be changed within nine months.

Not if you have any doubts about it.

This is certainly not the time for complacency.

Better stay where you are for the present.

Yes, if you change your present policy to some extent.

After much anxiety, peace of mind.

Yes, but this need not cause you any sleepless nights.

When you have almost ceased to hope, it will materialise.

This depends on someone you have yet to meet.

No, but your suspicions could cause a rift.

When you consider your income, your health and your interests, you will know the answer to this question.

You may recover it by a trick.

The removal of someone from your circle. A situation which will cause needless worry. The start of a lucky relationship.

Time arranges everything.

If you do not surrender today, you will tomorrow.

Confess if you must. The truth is bound to come out in any case.

The high areas of towns or cities are suitable for you; but avoid water, especially the sea.

Not if you are sensible.

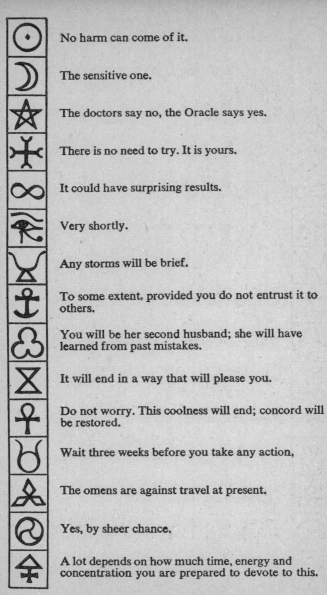

No harm can come of it.

The sensitive one.

The doctors say no, the Oracle says yes.

There is no need to try. It is yours.

It could have surprising results.

Very shortly.

Any storms will be brief.

To some extent, provided you do not entrust it to others.

You will be her second husband; she will have learned from past mistakes.

It will end in a way that will please you.

Do not worry. This coolness will end; concord will be restored.

Wait three weeks before you take any action.

The omens are against travel at present.

Yes, by sheer chance.

A lot depends on how much time, energy and concentration you are prepared to devote to this.

By not trying so hard.

Some praise lavishly; others criticise.

This would only pave the way to more trials and tribulations.

More than one long-distance trip; and very eventful.

Of your last meeting.

It has never been a secret.

It will be an improvement, in certain ways, on your younger days.

Beware of impatience.

You will be his second wife; he will be very devoted to you.

Do not seek for love. Let it find you.

You are doing the best you can in the circumstances.

Yes; you will have no cause to regret this.

Perhaps too young.

You may have complete faith in this.

Yes, provided certain conditions are modified.

You must be joking!

You will have cause to congratulate yourself.

They will think you are making a mistake, but hope for the best.

Courage! A stout heart will overcome them.

It is foolish to fear without cause.

He regrets that he has not more to offer you.

There are signs of a change within three months; and a greater one will follow it.

Yes.

Your talents are being wasted where you are. Make a change as quickly as possible.

Peace will be declared very shortly.

They were meant when they were spoken.

For various reasons, not all of them apparent, this person is greatly to be pitied. Show understanding, tolerance and kindness.

Make a few independent inquiries first.

If you are prepared to give up many things which are precious.

Very easily. Simply continue as you are doing now.

71

Out of sight, out of mind.

This can be arranged and will be to your satisfaction.

There may be certain advantages in going along with it.

As soon as possible.

Forgive, by all means; but be wiser in future.

That you are interesting.

This depends entirely on one circumstance.

In arts or crafts which will provide an outlet for your creative abilities.

You would be wise to keep an open mind about this until you receive more definite information.

Ignore any rumours to the contrary.

You will discover a mistake. Rewards for past efforts. A spur-of-the-moment decision will turn out right.

If you can curb that possessive streak.

More than you will care to recall.

An embroidered version of it.

Enquire again on the night following the next Full Moon.

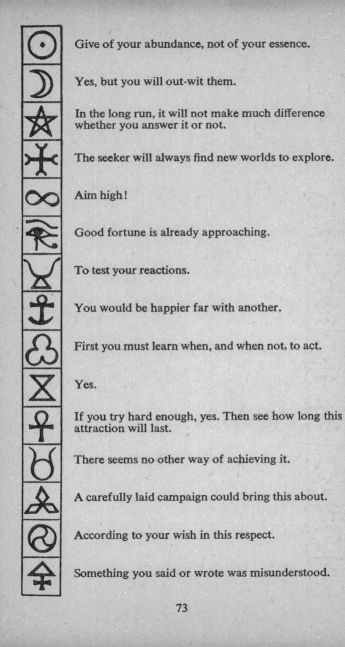

Give of your abundance, not of your essence.

Yes, but you will out-wit them.

In the long run, it will not make much difference whether you answer it or not.

The seeker will always find new worlds to explore.

Aim high!

Good fortune is already approaching.

To test your reactions.

You would be happier far with another.

First you must learn when, and when not, to act.

Yes.

If you try hard enough, yes. Then see how long this attraction will last.

There seems no other way of achieving it.

A carefully laid campaign could bring this about.

According to your wish in this respect.

Something you said or wrote was misunderstood.

73

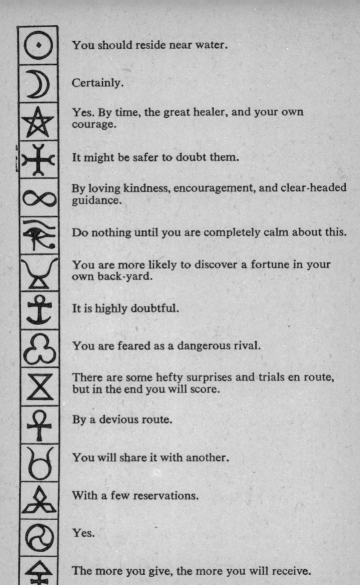	You should reside near water.
	Certainly.
	Yes. By time, the great healer, and your own courage.
	It might be safer to doubt them.
	By loving kindness, encouragement, and clear-headed guidance.
	Do nothing until you are completely calm about this.
	You are more likely to discover a fortune in your own back-yard.
	It is highly doubtful.
	You are feared as a dangerous rival.
	There are some hefty surprises and trials en route, but in the end you will score.
	By a devious route.
	You will share it with another.
	With a few reservations.
	Yes.
	The more you give, the more you will receive.

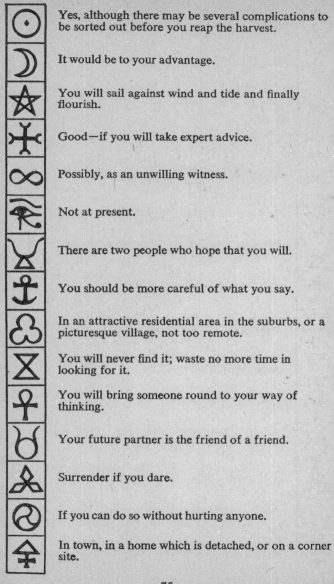

Yes, although there may be several complications to be sorted out before you reap the harvest.

It would be to your advantage.

You will sail against wind and tide and finally flourish.

Good—if you will take expert advice.

Possibly, as an unwilling witness.

Not at present.

There are two people who hope that you will.

You should be more careful of what you say.

In an attractive residential area in the suburbs, or a picturesque village, not too remote.

You will never find it; waste no more time in looking for it.

You will bring someone round to your way of thinking.

Your future partner is the friend of a friend.

Surrender if you dare.

If you can do so without hurting anyone.

In town, in a home which is detached, or on a corner site.

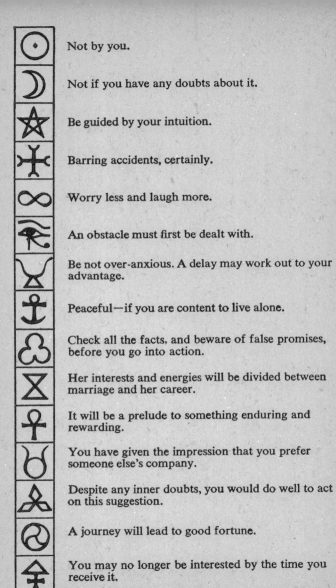

Not by you.

Not if you have any doubts about it.

Be guided by your intuition.

Barring accidents, certainly.

Worry less and laugh more.

An obstacle must first be dealt with.

Be not over-anxious. A delay may work out to your advantage.

Peaceful—if you are content to live alone.

Check all the facts, and beware of false promises, before you go into action.

Her interests and energies will be divided between marriage and her career.

It will be a prelude to something enduring and rewarding.

You have given the impression that you prefer someone else's company.

Despite any inner doubts, you would do well to act on this suggestion.

A journey will lead to good fortune.

You may no longer be interested by the time you receive it.

In a limited field, yes.

You cannot please everyone.

That there is something intriguing about you.

If you are prepared to shoulder most of the work and responsibility.

During the next seven years, yes.

Serious thoughts about the future.

People believe what you want them to believe.

As you have sown, so shall you reap.

If you can recognise love when you meet it.

He is quietly-spoken, sturdily-built and wears a ring on his little finger.

A dream will give you the answer to this question.

Judge by the results you have had over the last year.

You have discovered a jewel. Cherish it.

Some time must elapse before the wedding-date is fixed.

At present, which is perhaps more than can be said about the future.

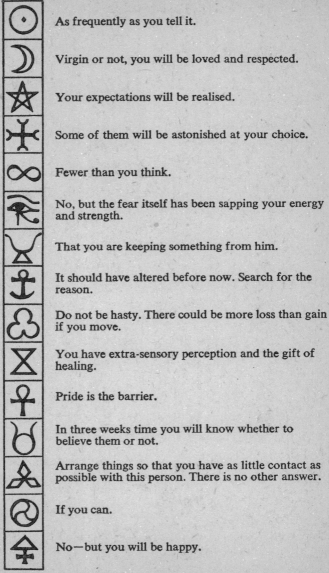

As frequently as you tell it.

Virgin or not, you will be loved and respected.

Your expectations will be realised.

Some of them will be astonished at your choice.

Fewer than you think.

No, but the fear itself has been sapping your energy and strength.

That you are keeping something from him.

It should have altered before now. Search for the reason.

Do not be hasty. There could be more loss than gain if you move.

You have extra-sensory perception and the gift of healing.

Pride is the barrier.

In three weeks time you will know whether to believe them or not.

Arrange things so that you have as little contact as possible with this person. There is no other answer.

If you can.

No—but you will be happy.

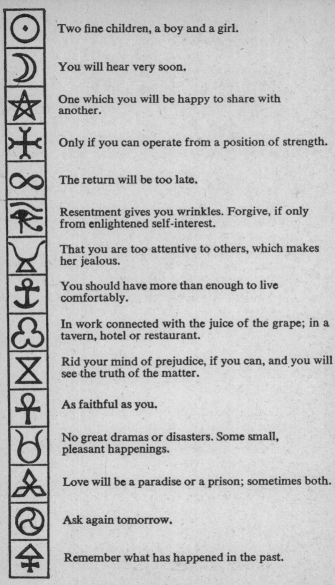

Two fine children, a boy and a girl.

You will hear very soon.

One which you will be happy to share with another.

Only if you can operate from a position of strength.

The return will be too late.

Resentment gives you wrinkles. Forgive, if only from enlightened self-interest.

That you are too attentive to others, which makes her jealous.

You should have more than enough to live comfortably.

In work connected with the juice of the grape; in a tavern, hotel or restaurant.

Rid your mind of prejudice, if you can, and you will see the truth of the matter.

As faithful as you.

No great dramas or disasters. Some small, pleasant happenings.

Love will be a paradise or a prison; sometimes both.

Ask again tomorrow.

Remember what has happened in the past.

Long enough to discover that your heart should have been set elsewhere.

It is difficult for you to refuse.

A person who is gifted in any way must always expect to have rivals.

Leave it aside for a week. Then you will know what to write.

Until the evening of life, which will be spent in peaceful retirement.

Feel, think, speak and act positively.

It may seem long to you, but in fact it will not last much longer.

Through sheer forgetfulness.

If you can take off your rose-tinted spectacles, you will see that the answer is no.

Be prepared for some difficulties and losses at first; after which you will be fortunate.

Your friend has already been told by someone else.

It seems unlikely at the moment.

Yes.

Happy and fruitful—but hardly wealthy.

One within the first year of marriage, certainly.

No. This would be sheer self-indulgence.

A cottage in the country and a place in town would be ideal for you.

If there is the slightest doubt, abandon the idea.

You have not much longer to endure.

They are sincere.

By not interfering. Your friend will learn from this experience.

Yes.

It would be better to wait three months before you make a definite decision on this.

It cannot and should not last.

You have hurt this person's feelings in some way.

Yes, if you can stand the pace.

This might cause more pain than profit.

It has been willed to you and revoked, but you may yet inherit.

There is no reason to doubt it.

No; but you will have no reason to complain.

Success lies close to home.

This will depend on a whim.

Within the year.

For each reverse, you will have two successes.

Someone, possibly yourself, bars the way to a solution.

Simply to protect your own interests.

You may depend upon it.

Someone may need a bit of encouragement.

No; something you said or did was misunderstood.

You will thrive best in an airy, elevated location; mountain or ranching country, where there are no restrictions.

You will not find it; be more circumspect in future.

You will cover new ground, and gain thereby. Recompense will be made for something which happened in the past.

It is uncertain.

Should you break if off, you will have the pleasure of a reconciliation.

Do nothing for the moment.

If you must.

Your friend says yes, the Oracle says no.

Accept it by all means.

A third person has yet to be considered.

Your ills will be mostly imaginary.

The less effort you make, the easier it will be.

Not without serious thought and consideration of all the factors involved.

A benign and friendly planet promises good and speedy tidings.

You will play the role of peace-maker when others raise a storm.

Yes, to your fullest satisfaction.

A beautiful, true and faithful spouse will grace your dwelling.

It may end—and begin all over again.

It will be better for you if it continues.

If you act in haste, you may regret it.

There should be no necessity for you to seek riches abroad.

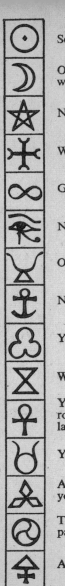

Seek another opinion first.

Over-night fame will in fact be preceded by much work and some setbacks.

Nothing can please some people. Give up.

What you deserve.

Got it alone, until a more suitable partner appears.

Not yet, and not very much.

Of someone you both know.

Not during your lifetime.

You have much to look forward to.

Why should you doubt it?

You will reject a host of admirers and marry a rough diamond, whose integrity will compensate for lack of polish.

Yes.

A wider outlet for your energies could be found if you look for it.

This might cost you more than you are prepared to pay.

Are you not already married in a sense?

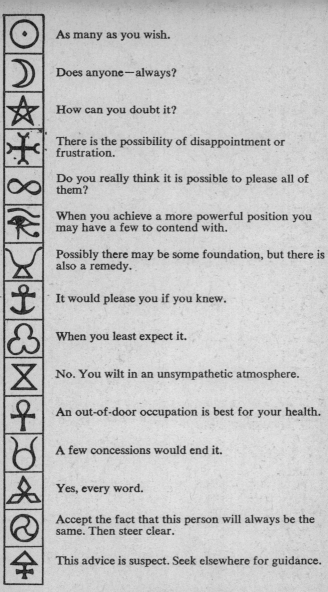

As many as you wish.

Does anyone—always?

How can you doubt it?

There is the possibility of disappointment or frustration.

Do you really think it is possible to please all of them?

When you achieve a more powerful position you may have a few to contend with.

Possibly there may be some foundation, but there is also a remedy.

It would please you if you knew.

When you least expect it.

No. You wilt in an unsympathetic atmosphere.

An out-of-door occupation is best for your health.

A few concessions would end it.

Yes, every word.

Accept the fact that this person will always be the same. Then steer clear.

This advice is suspect. Seek elsewhere for guidance.

Yes, if you are prepared to pay the price.

Twins!]

To give you more time to think.

Yes. Influences of which you are unaware at present will bring this about.

If you are prepared for a battle, yes.

It is not a matter of choice.

No harm was intended. Forgive freely.

That she will be true to you, if you will be true to her.

Live in hope!

An occupation of an intellectual and humanitarian type, such as medicine, education, social welfare, politics.

Do not take any action until your suspicions are proved.

That is asking a great deal.

A weight will be taken off your mind. A conversation will start you thinking along new lines. A windfall.

If you choose wisely.

As many again as you have had already.

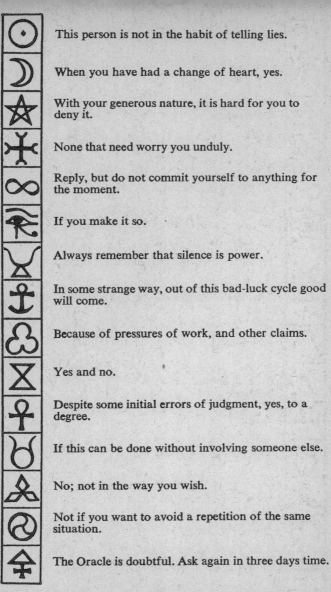

This person is not in the habit of telling lies.

When you have had a change of heart, yes.

With your generous nature, it is hard for you to deny it.

None that need worry you unduly.

Reply, but do not commit yourself to anything for the moment.

If you make it so.

Always remember that silence is power.

In some strange way, out of this bad-luck cycle good will come.

Because of pressures of work, and other claims.

Yes and no.

Despite some initial errors of judgment, yes, to a degree.

If this can be done without involving someone else.

No; not in the way you wish.

Not if you want to avoid a repetition of the same situation.

The Oracle is doubtful. Ask again in three days time.

Break it off—if you can.

Yes, but be careful to choose the right moment.

Live where you feel most at home.

There are more than just two people to be considered in this affair.

Yes, when you realise that change is part of the pattern of life. Your best times are still to come.

Promises, like pie-crust, can be broken.

They also serve who only stand and wait for the call for help.

You are certainly entitled to one, but whether you will get it is another matter.

It would give you more outlet and opportunity than you have here.

When it ends, you will have no regrets.

There is a feeling of resentment, possibly because of your good fortune.

Yes, if you map out a programme and stick to it.

In the not too distant future, you will be in full possession of the facts.

If you are prepared to make some sacrifices for it.

Take nothing for granted until it is proved.

A change for the better.

Across water.

Yes.

Various indications point in that direction.

Better organisation is needed.

Great and permanent benefits.

The chances are three to one against this ever happening.

You will have what you deserve.

You have already missed one chance. See you do not miss another.

Something you said has been twisted, certainly.

In a village which is close to a city so you can enjoy the pleasures of both.

You will never see it again; you must be more careful.

A decision will be made which will affect your life for many years to come.

You might regret it, if you do.

Have you the strength to break it off?

89

If you place loyalty before intelligence, yes.

Young enough, but still not young enough to satisfy you.

True friendship is rare, but you may safely place your trust in this one.

No. There is a better one on the way.

The one whose absence you would feel most.

You can expect health, joy and prosperity.

There are others who are equally interested in the matter.

Some re-thinking is necessary before you proceed.

An obstacle intervenes for a time.

Far from peaceful.

The Oracle predicts ultimate success, if due care and prudence are taken.

The woman destined to be your bride is talkative, lively and a very good cook.

Live one day at a time.

A policy of expediency is being followed.

The best of good luck.

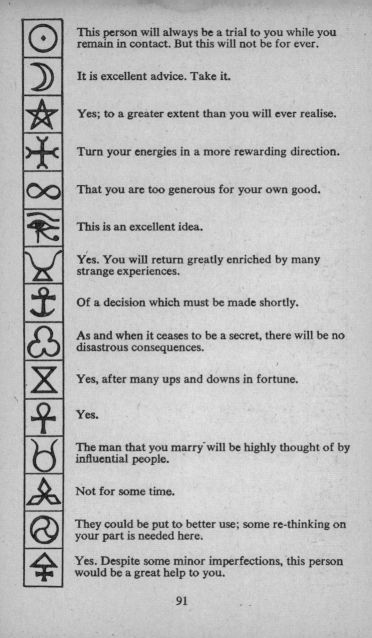

This person will always be a trial to you while you remain in contact. But this will not be for ever.

It is excellent advice. Take it.

Yes; to a greater extent than you will ever realise.

Turn your energies in a more rewarding direction.

That you are too generous for your own good.

This is an excellent idea.

Yes. You will return greatly enriched by many strange experiences.

Of a decision which must be made shortly.

As and when it ceases to be a secret, there will be no disastrous consequences.

Yes, after many ups and downs in fortune.

Yes.

The man that you marry will be highly thought of by influential people.

Not for some time.

They could be put to better use; some re-thinking on your part is needed here.

Yes. Despite some minor imperfections, this person would be a great help to you.

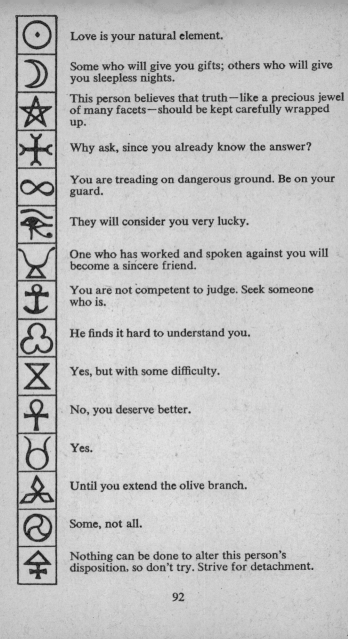

Love is your natural element.

Some who will give you gifts; others who will give you sleepless nights.

This person believes that truth—like a precious jewel of many facets—should be kept carefully wrapped up.

Why ask, since you already know the answer?

You are treading on dangerous ground. Be on your guard.

They will consider you very lucky.

One who has worked and spoken against you will become a sincere friend.

You are not competent to judge. Seek someone who is.

He finds it hard to understand you.

Yes, but with some difficulty.

No, you deserve better.

Yes.

Until you extend the olive branch.

Some, not all.

Nothing can be done to alter this person's disposition, so don't try. Strive for detachment.

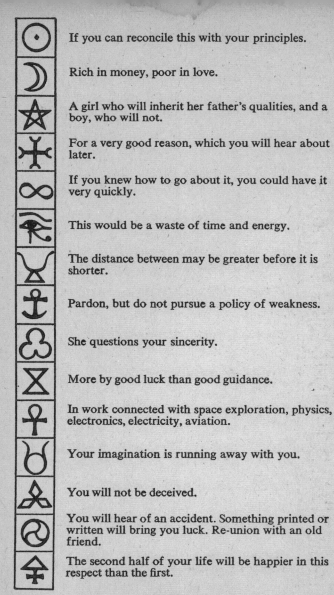

If you can reconcile this with your principles.

Rich in money, poor in love.

A girl who will inherit her father's qualities, and a boy, who will not.

For a very good reason, which you will hear about later.

If you knew how to go about it, you could have it very quickly.

This would be a waste of time and energy.

The distance between may be greater before it is shorter.

Pardon, but do not pursue a policy of weakness.

She questions your sincerity.

More by good luck than good guidance.

In work connected with space exploration, physics, electronics, electricity, aviation.

Your imagination is running away with you.

You will not be deceived.

You will hear of an accident. Something printed or written will bring you luck. Re-union with an old friend.

The second half of your life will be happier in this respect than the first.

Yes. Had you behaved differently, it would be yours by now.

An unlikely story!

Yes, by an unexpected stroke of luck.

No.

Only one who constitutes a danger. Be on guard.

No answer is the best answer in this case.

Your path through life will be adventurous; strewn with rocks as well as roses.

Unruly emotions coupled with an unruly tongue spell failure. Exercise restraint.

You have not much longer to wait.

After a certain problem has been worked out, you will get it.

If you are prepared to make the necessary adjustments, yes.

If you can hold the image of success clearly in your mind, and dwell on it daily.

Keep it to yourself for the present.

Perhaps sooner than you think.

It would be to your advantage.

94

One that you know very well.

Why ask? If you break it off today, you will be together again tomorrow.

No. Discretion is your best policy where this matter is concerned.

The pressures of town life are not good for you. You should live in the country.

You have yet to meet the person you will marry.

Love will release you.

When they are signed and witnessed.

In the final analysis, your friend must work out this problem alone.

All the facts will slot into place without doing this.

You have already made up your mind about this.

You have little to lose if it breaks up.

This could be the result of your own neglect.

You will certainly make headway, but in doing so you will also make enemies.

In time, all will be revealed.

Your wish will be granted.

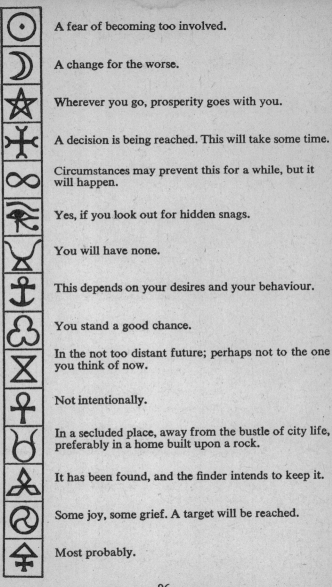

A fear of becoming too involved.

A change for the worse.

Wherever you go, prosperity goes with you.

A decision is being reached. This will take some time.

Circumstances may prevent this for a while, but it will happen.

Yes, if you look out for hidden snags.

You will have none.

This depends on your desires and your behaviour.

You stand a good chance.

In the not too distant future; perhaps not to the one you think of now.

Not intentionally.

In a secluded place, away from the bustle of city life, preferably in a home built upon a rock.

It has been found, and the finder intends to keep it.

Some joy, some grief. A target will be reached.

Most probably.

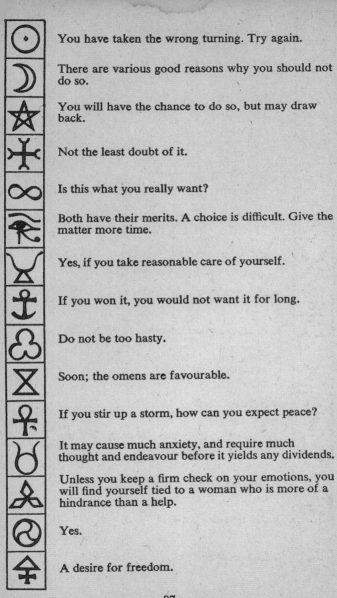

You have taken the wrong turning. Try again.

There are various good reasons why you should not do so.

You will have the chance to do so, but may draw back.

Not the least doubt of it.

Is this what you really want?

Both have their merits. A choice is difficult. Give the matter more time.

Yes, if you take reasonable care of yourself.

If you won it, you would not want it for long.

Do not be too hasty.

Soon; the omens are favourable.

If you stir up a storm, how can you expect peace?

It may cause much anxiety, and require much thought and endeavour before it yields any dividends.

Unless you keep a firm check on your emotions, you will find yourself tied to a woman who is more of a hindrance than a help.

Yes.

A desire for freedom.